miffy x rijksm

mercis x rijksmuseum

In this book, you'll find highlights from the Rijksmuseum's collection alongside drawings by Dick Bruna. See how Miffy and other characters compare to some of our most beloved artworks from different eras.

Take a fresh look at these firm favourites.
Enjoy them through the eyes of a child.
Can you spot the similarities and differences?

Most of the artworks in this book are on permanent display at the museum. Why not take Miffy along as you wander through the Rijksmuseum!

Miffy is dressed up as a ghost. Boo!
The swan is puffing and flapping. Watch out!
How do you scare people?

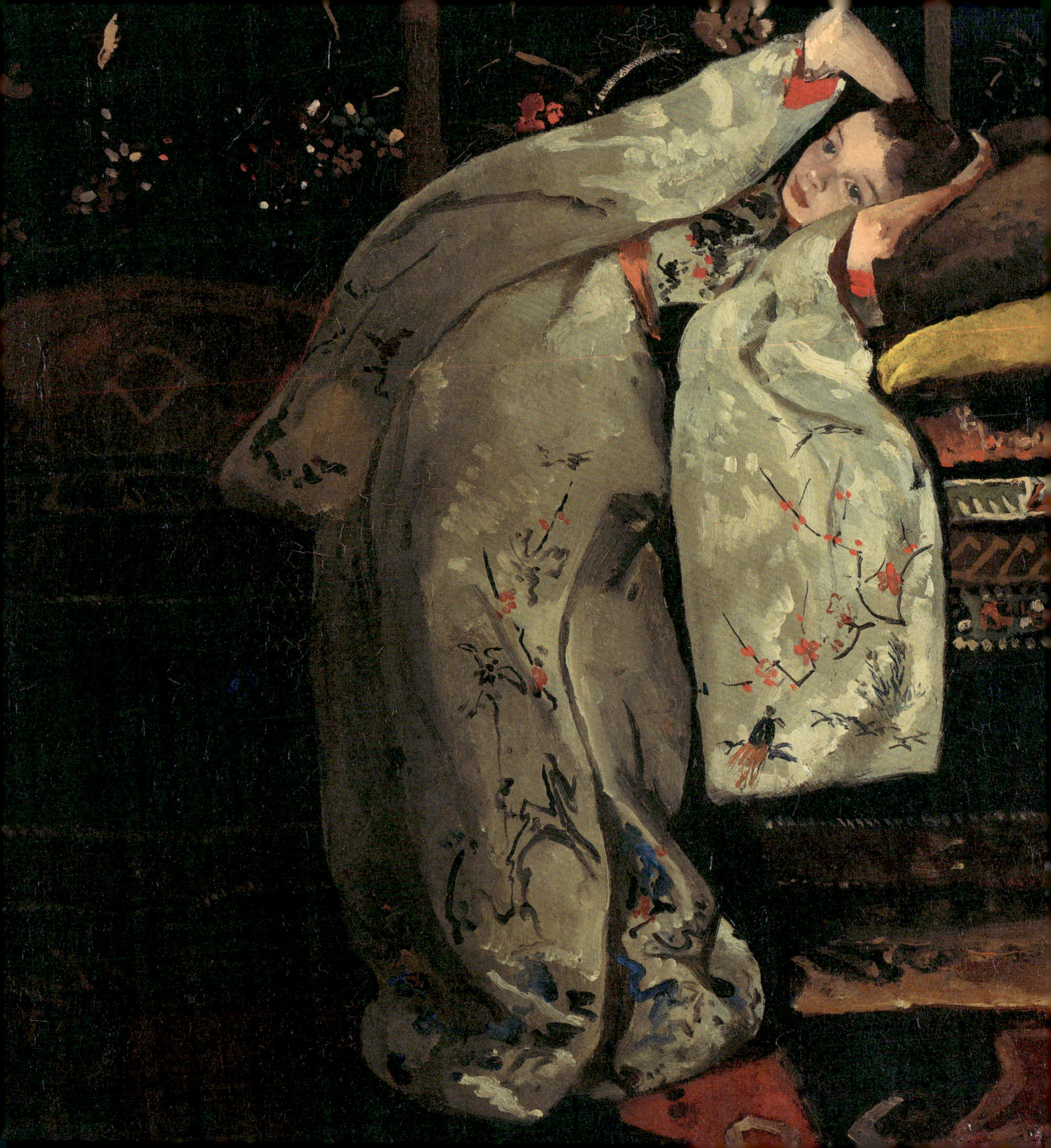

The girl in the painting and Miffy are
both wearing beautiful kimonos.
Do you see the pretty flowers?

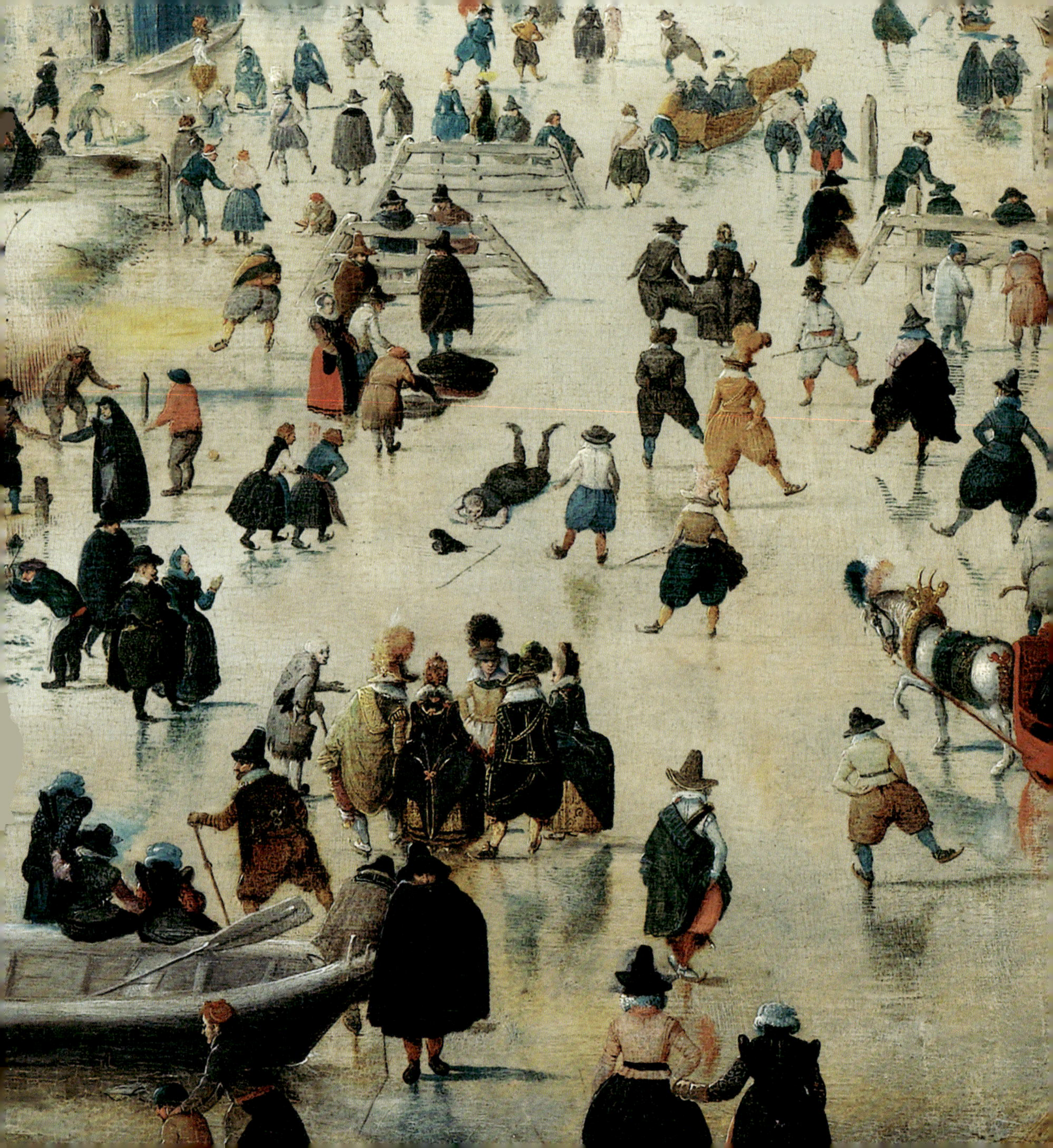

Miffy loves ice skating in winter.
Look at all the skaters in the painting.
What else is going on?

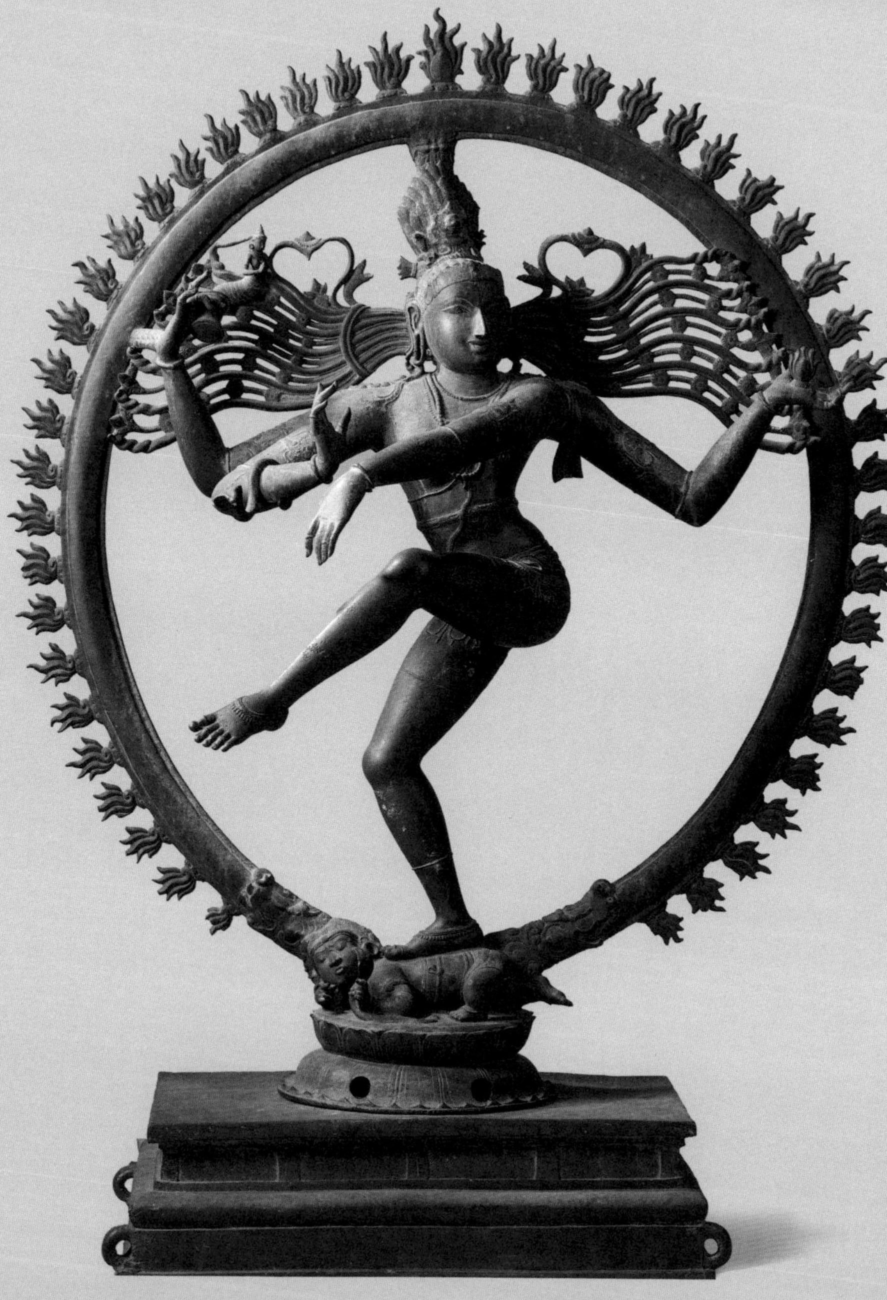

Have you tried dancing on one leg,
with your hands in the air?
Wow, that's impressive!

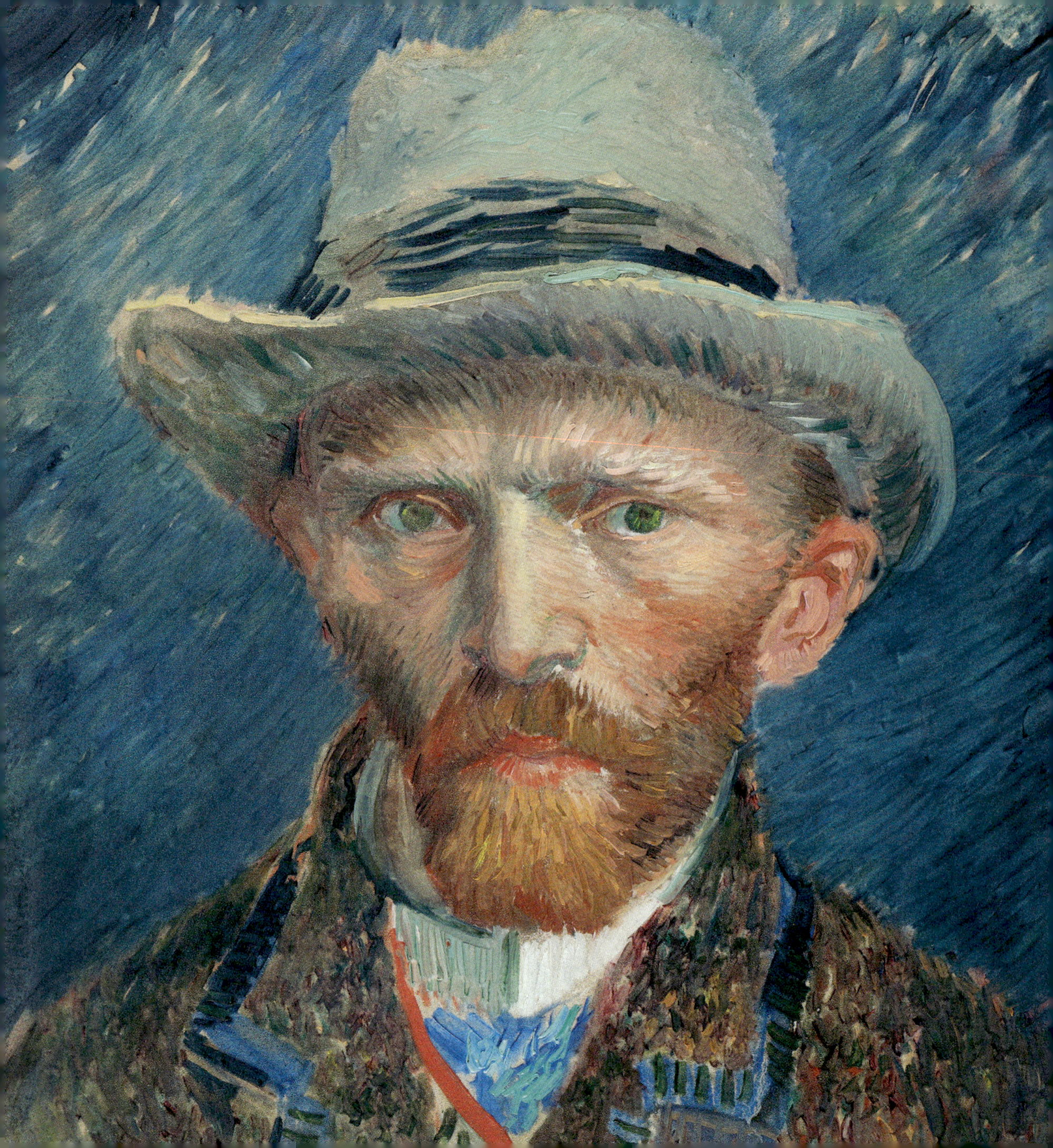

**A self-portrait is a drawing or painting of yourself.
It's a bit like looking in the mirror.
Why not draw your own self-portrait!**

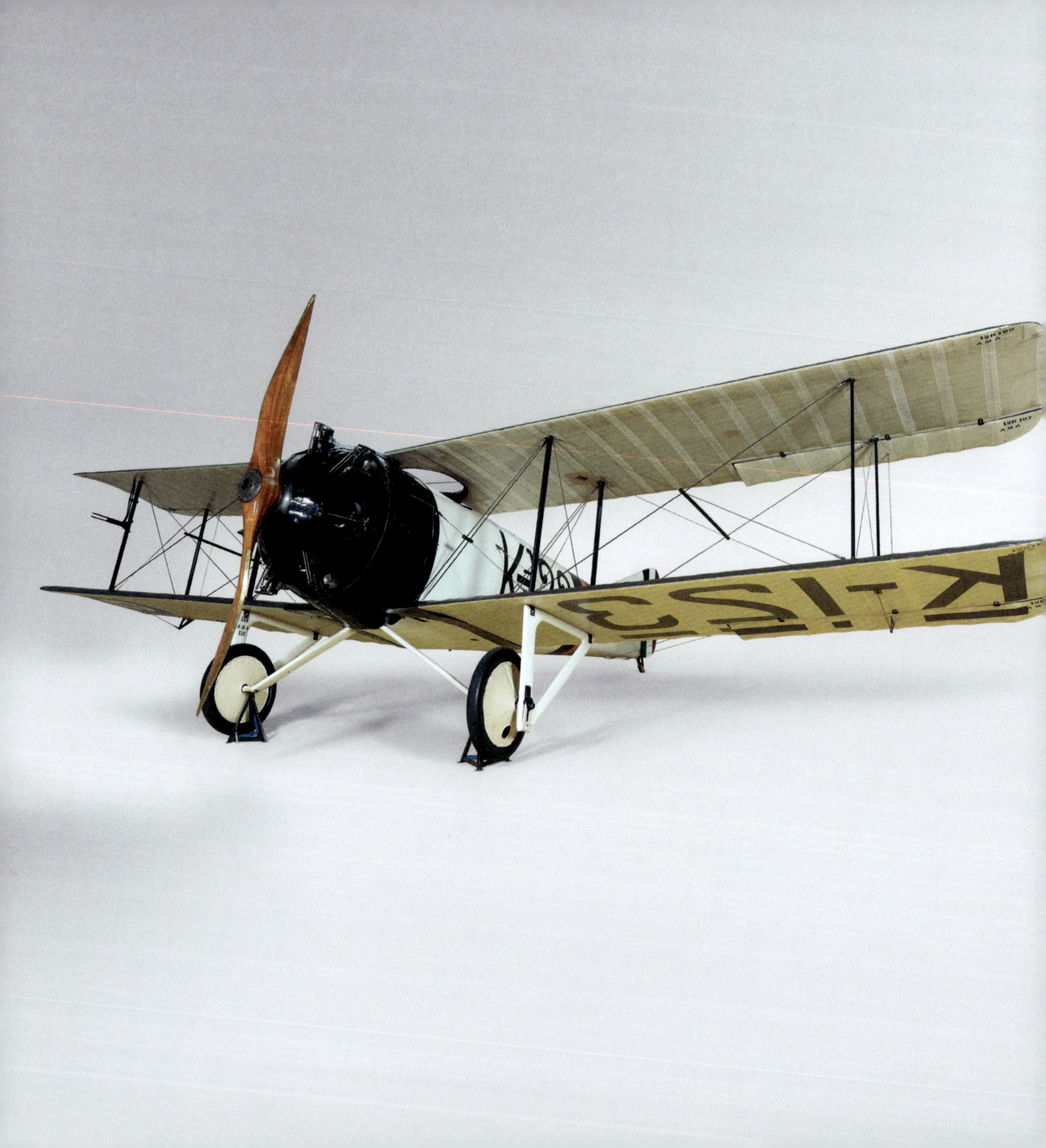

Uncle Pilot takes Miffy up high
on an adventure in his plane.
Where would you fly to?

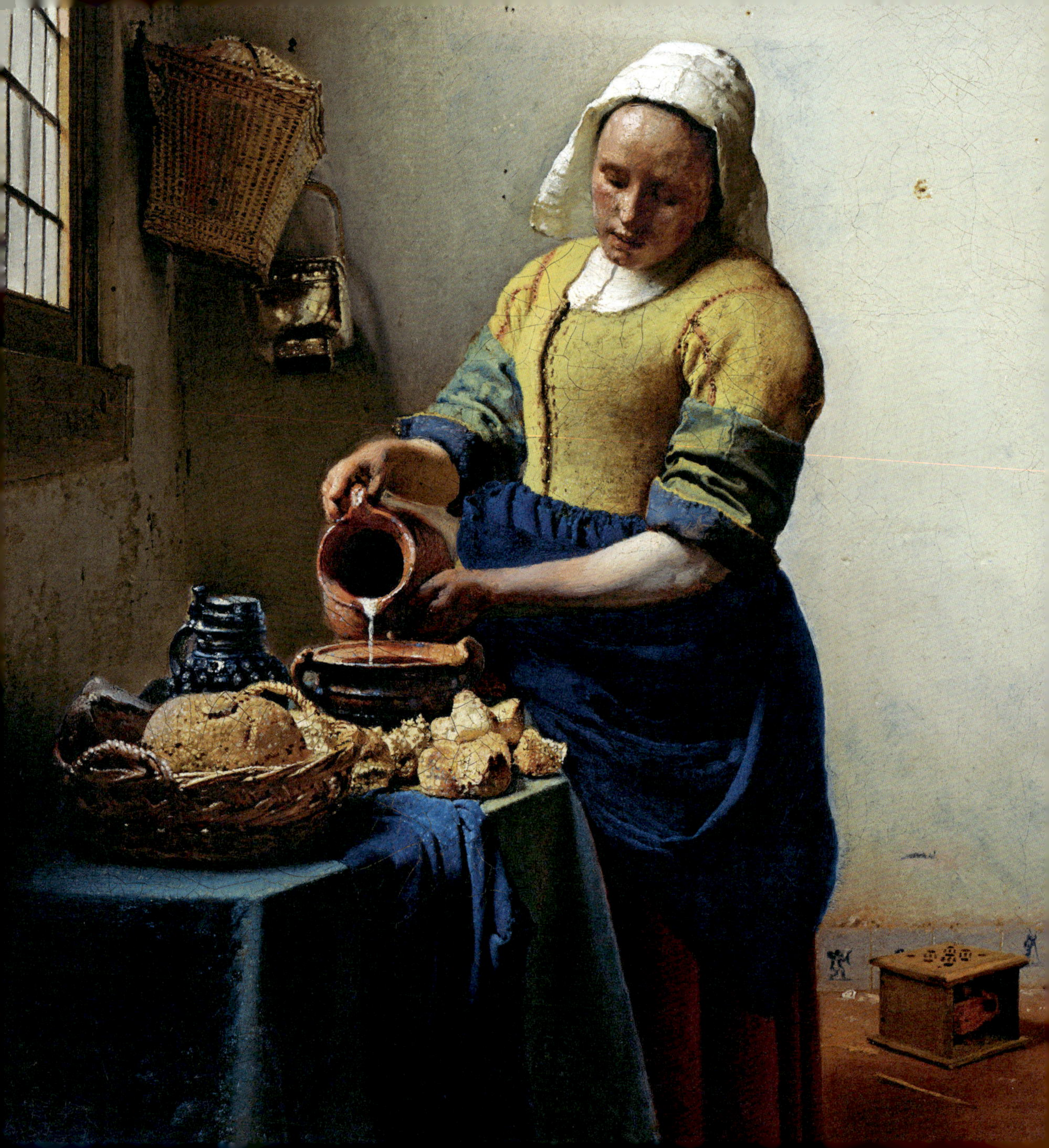

**Miffy is watering the pretty flowers.
What is the girl in the painting doing?**

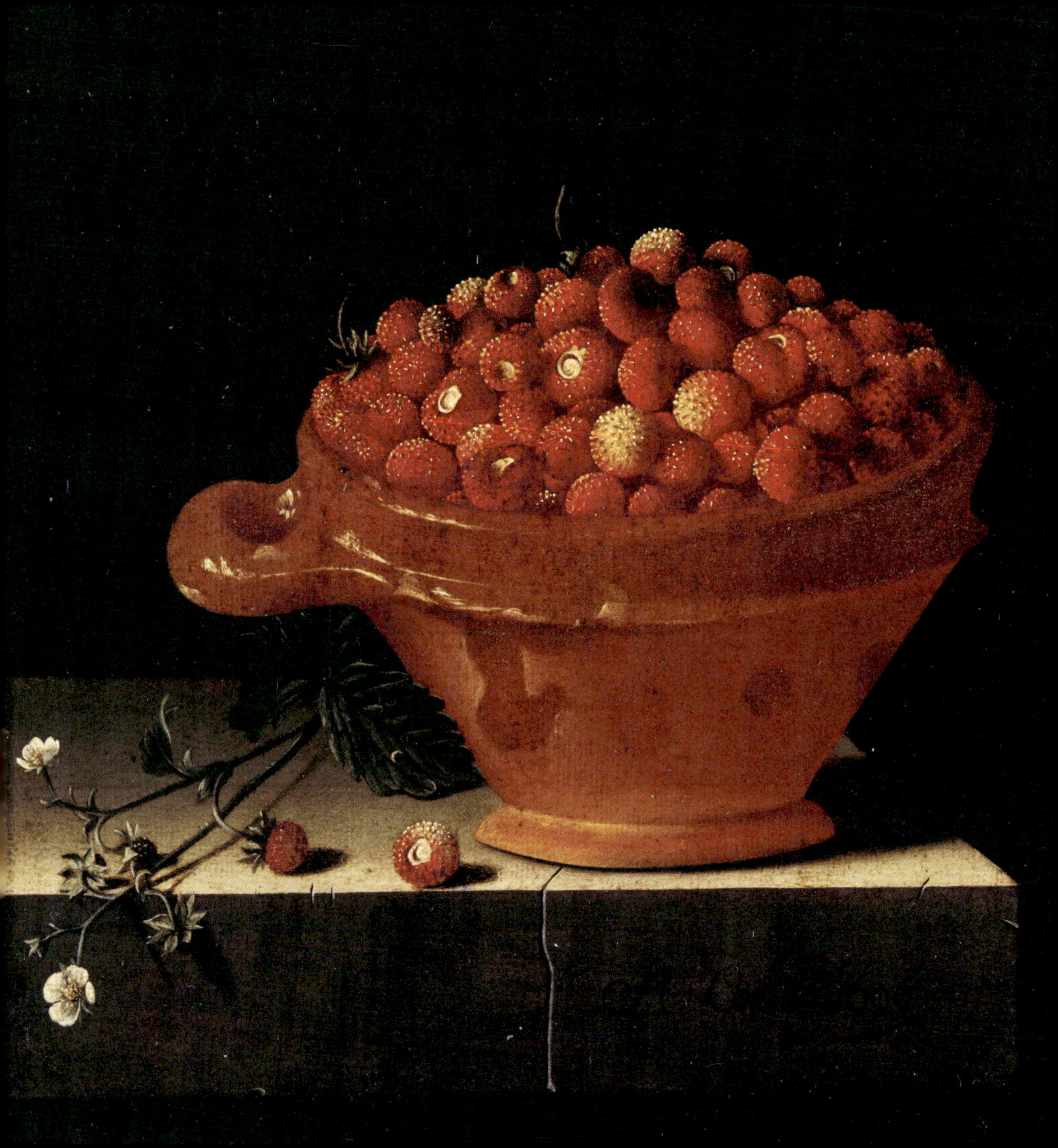

**These strawberries look good enough to eat!
What's your favourite fruit?**

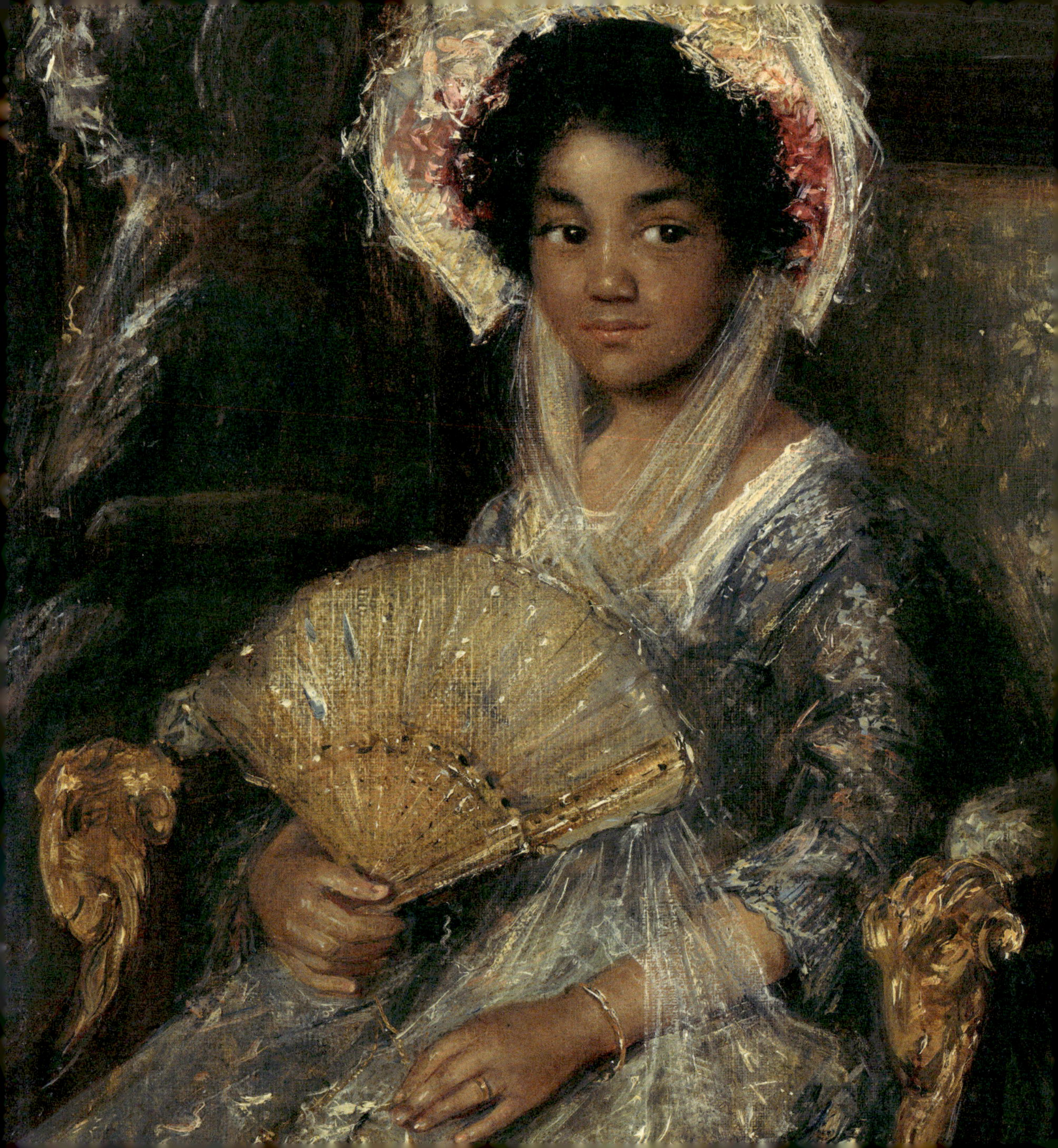

**Isabella and Miffy are looking very festive.
Where could they be going?**

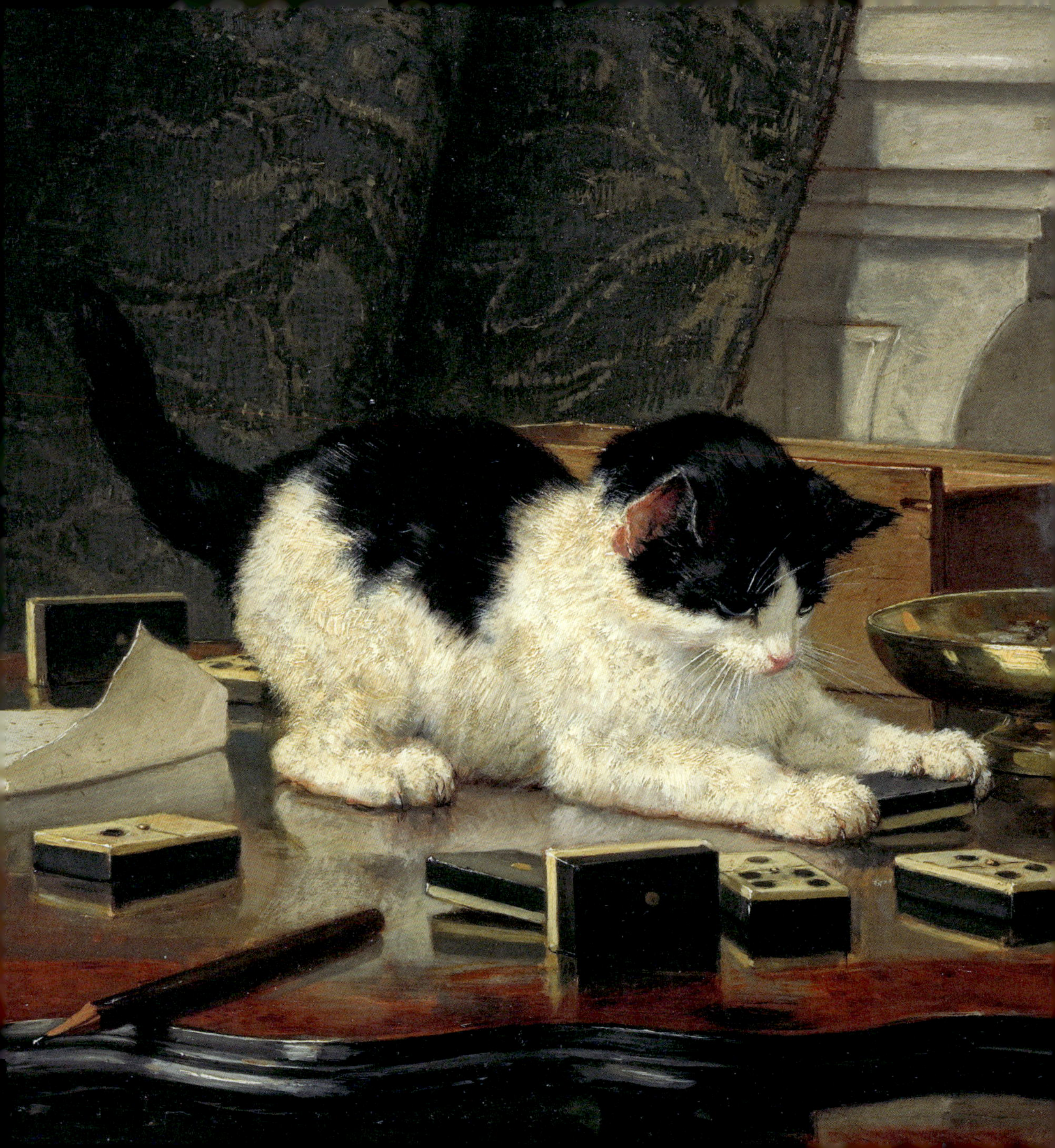

**Miaow!
What is the cat doing on the desk?**

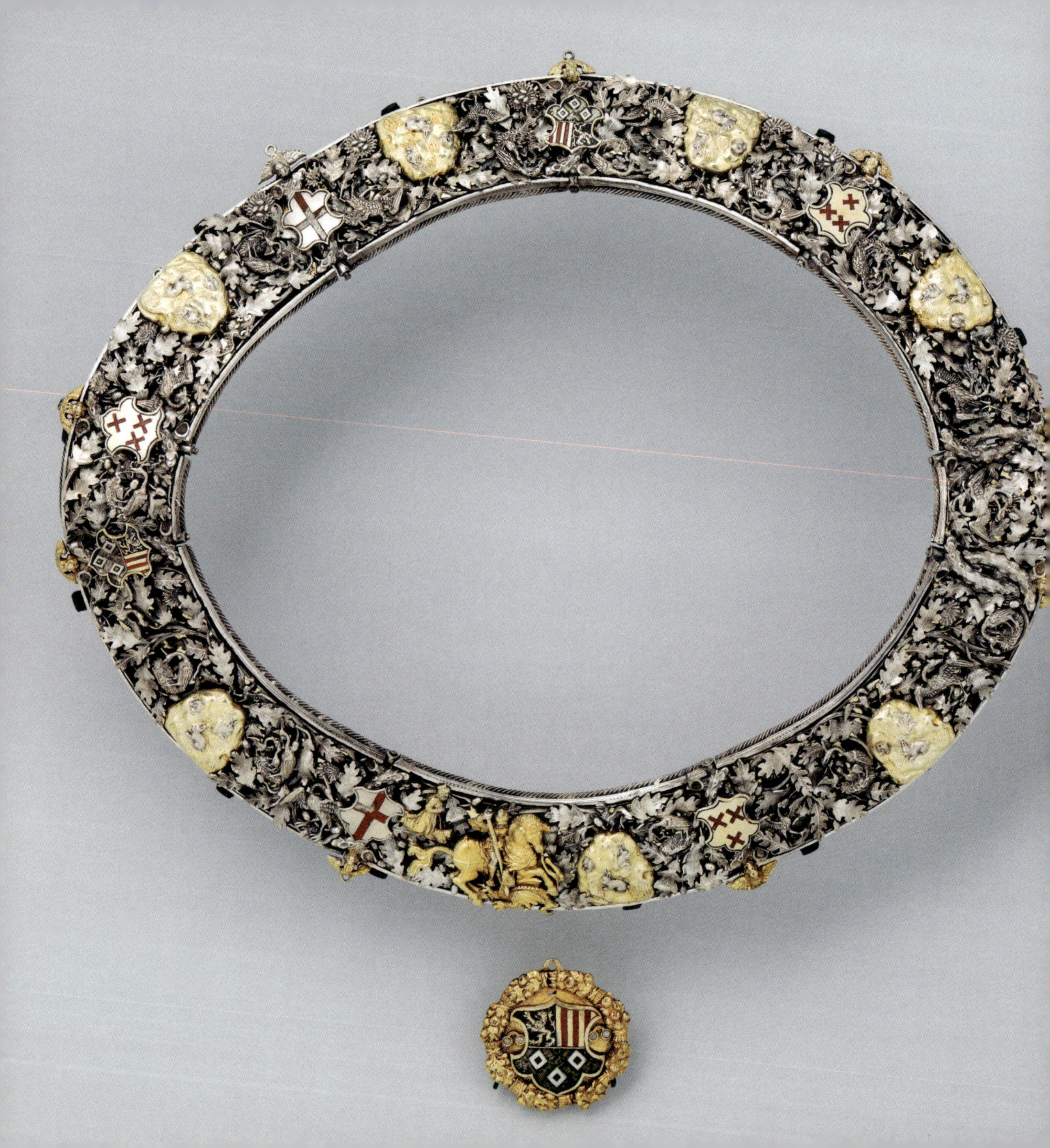

Such a decorative chain!
It looks lovely on the mayor.

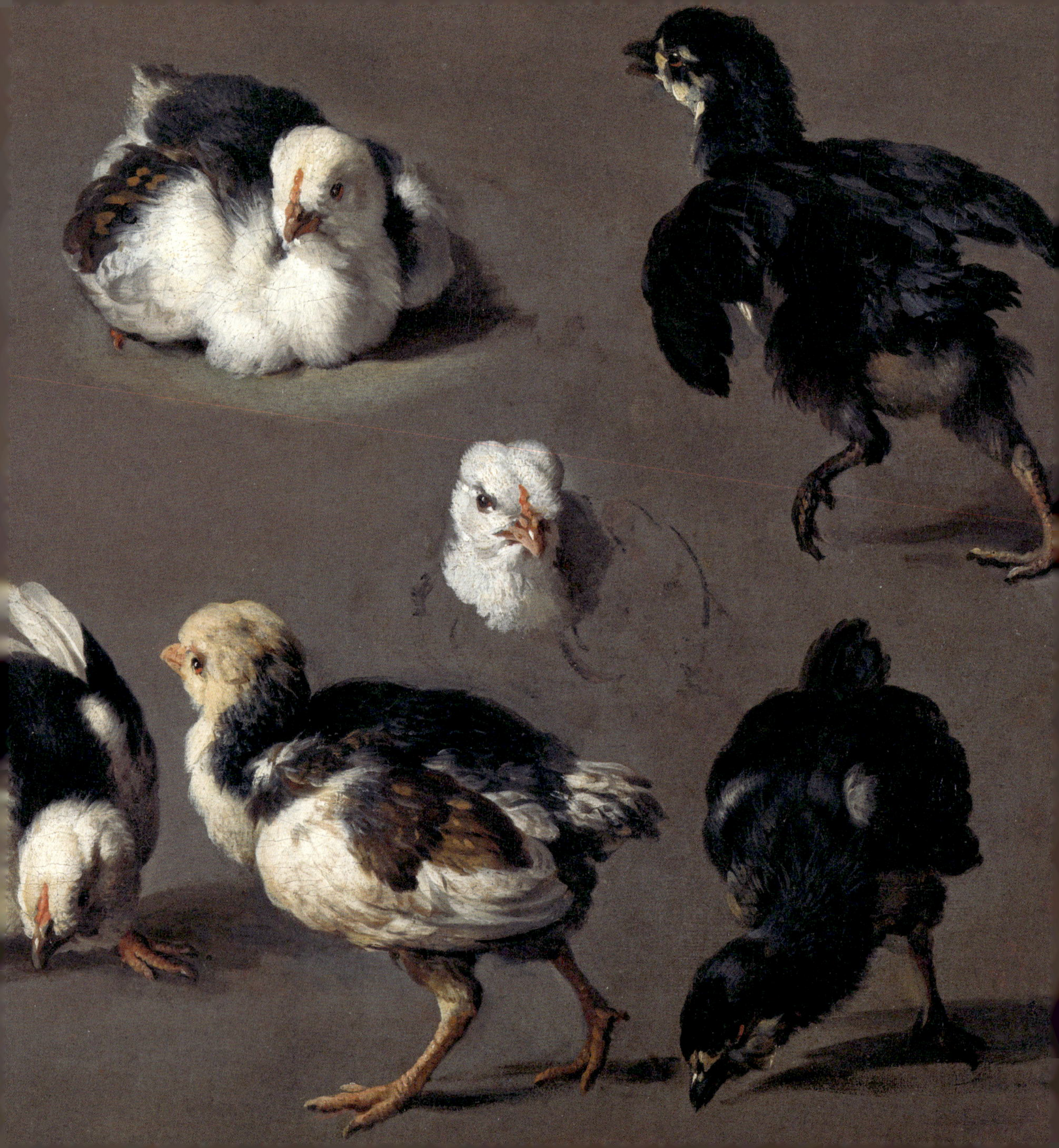

**What a lot of chicks!
Can you count them?**

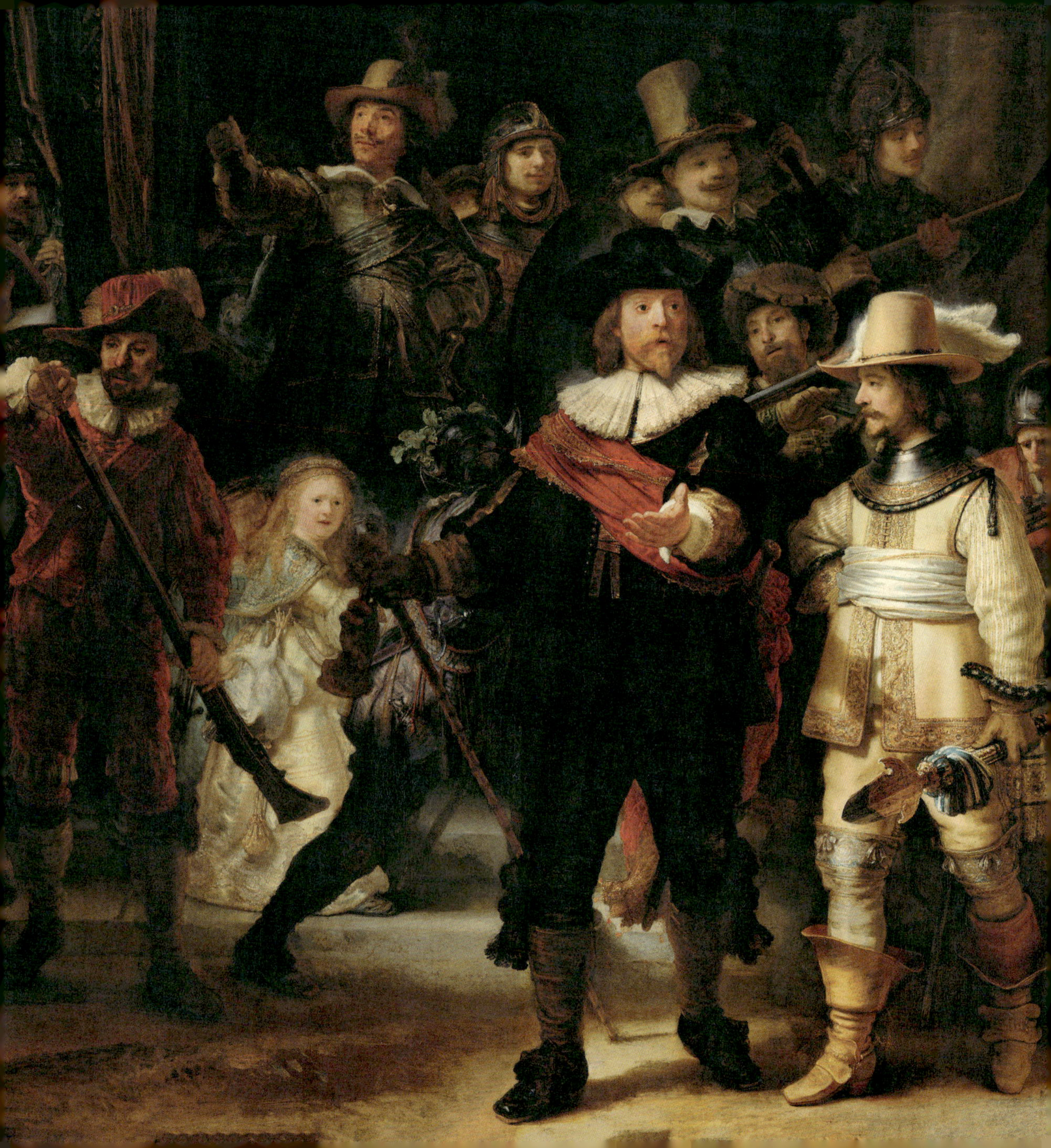

Who did you look at first?
Was it the colour of their clothes?
Or their place in the picture?

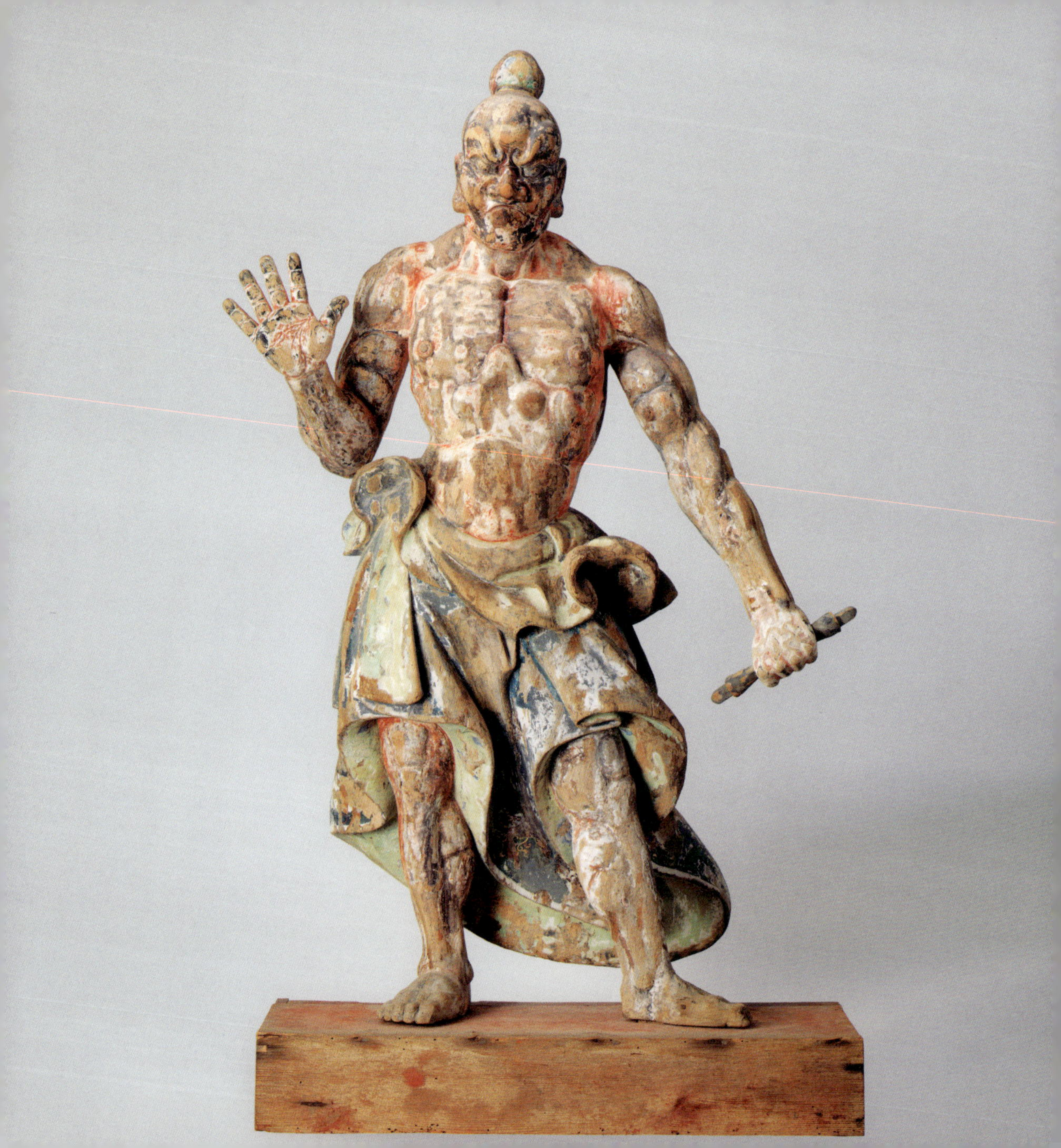

Halt! These guards make sure that no one just walks in. Would you stop?

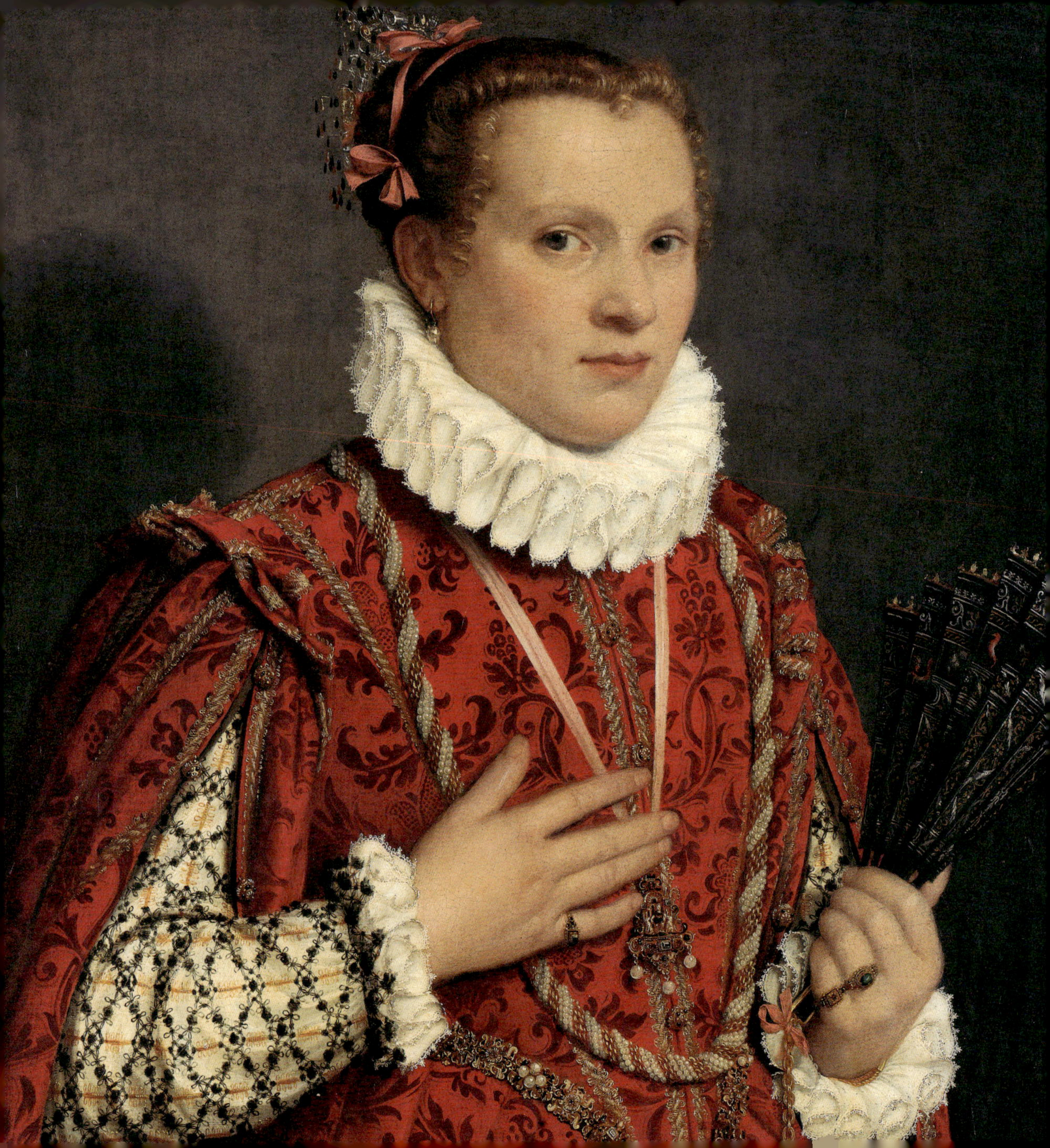

**Poppy is taking a picture. Click!
The girl has put on her finest dress.
How would you dress up for a photo?**

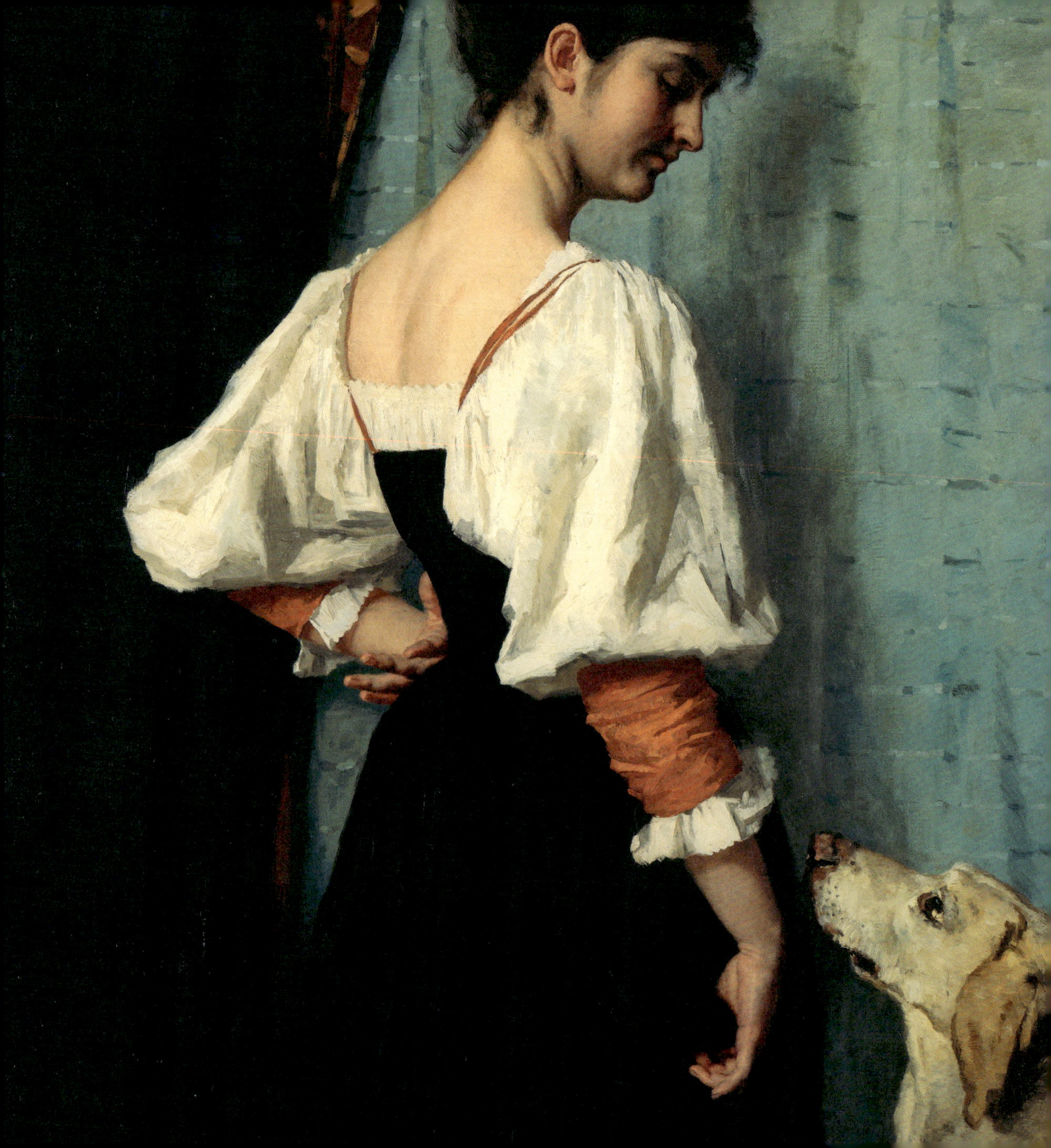

Miffy gives Snuffy a treat.
Does Puck in the painting also deserve one?

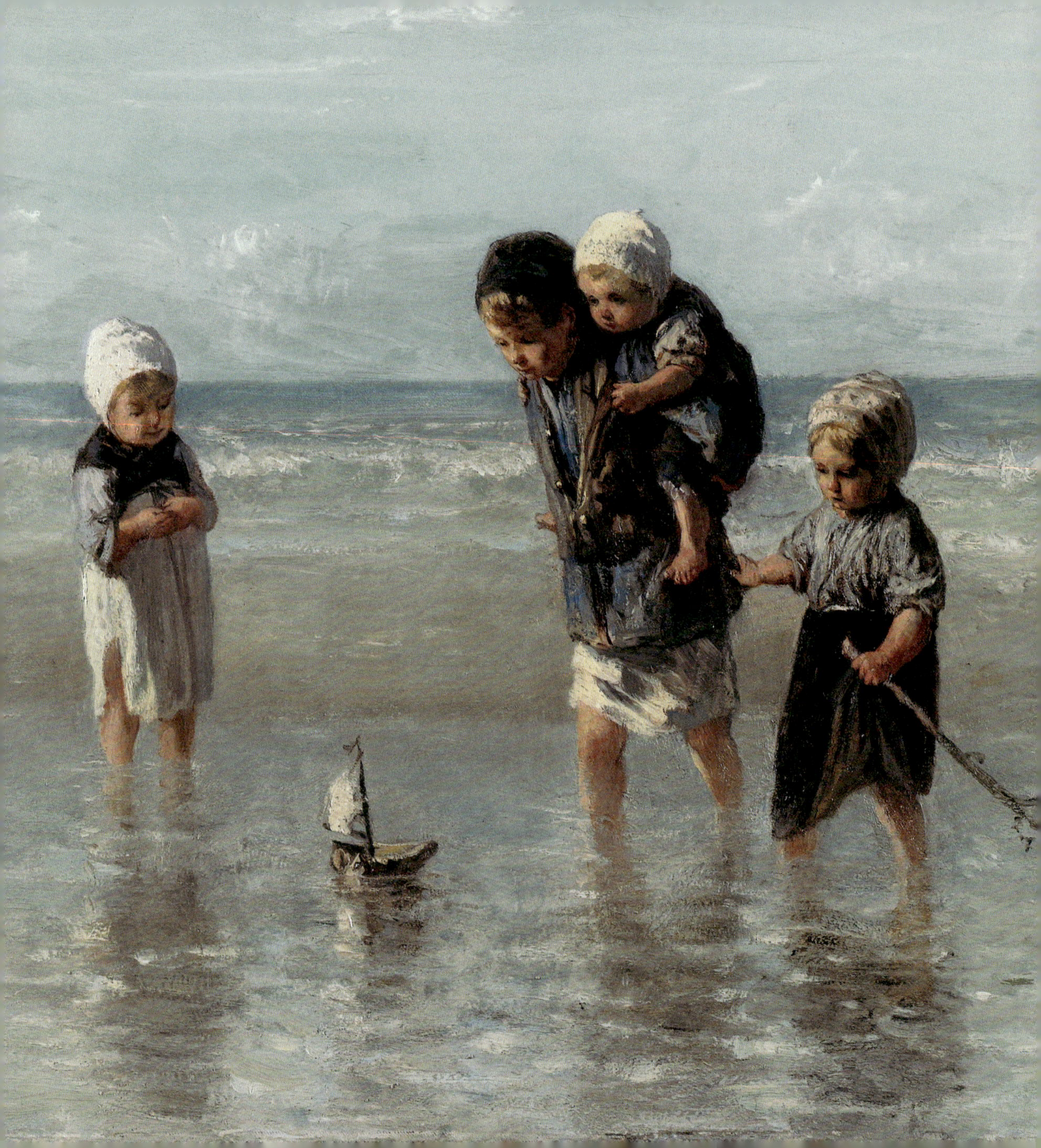

The children are sailing a little ship.
Miffy is digging a hole in the sand.
What do you enjoy doing at the beach?

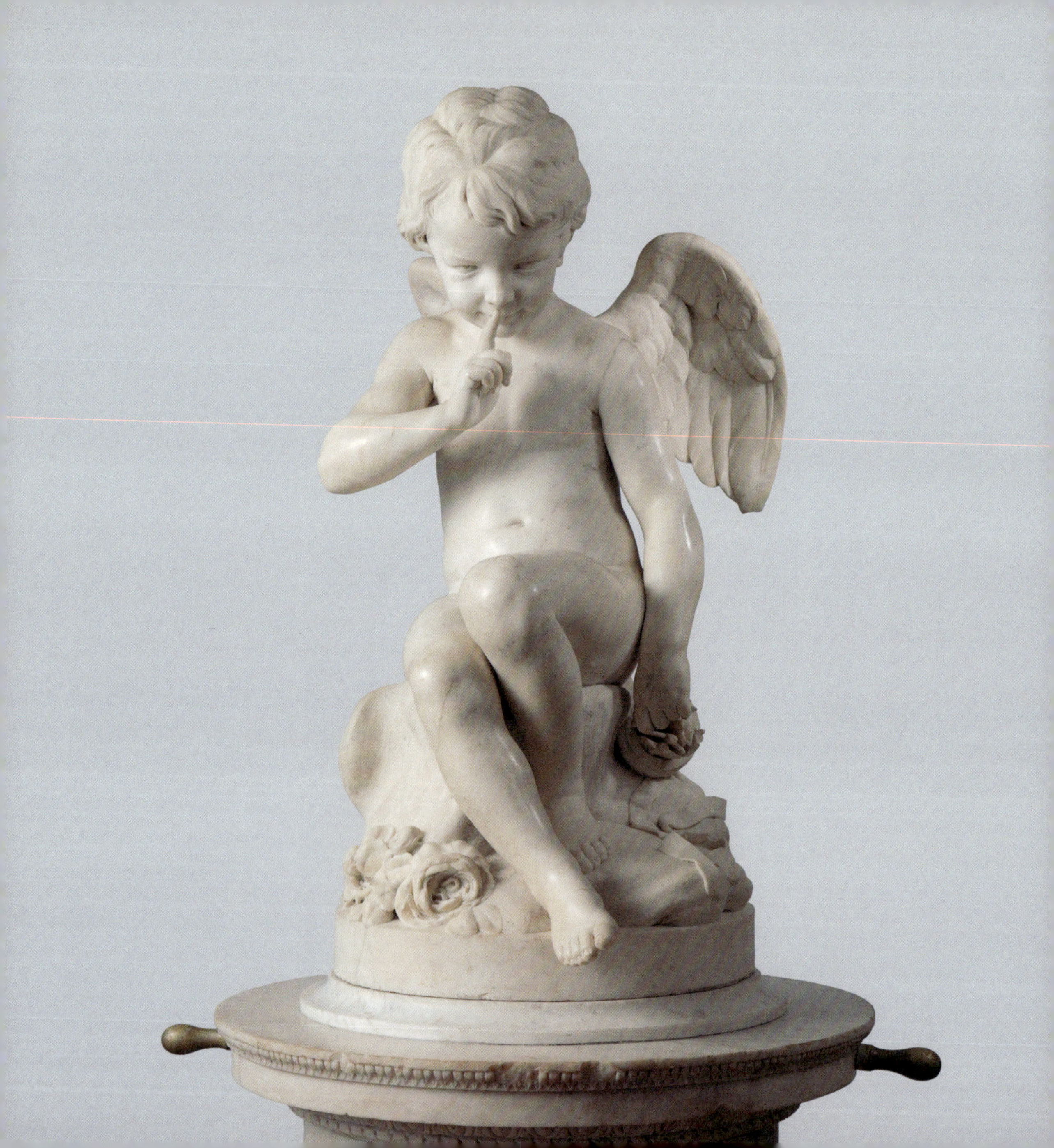

**Shh! Be as quiet as a mouse.
What do you hear around you?**

Illustrations

Jan Asselijn, 'The Threatened Swan', c. 1650; Rijksmuseum, Amsterdam.
Dick Bruna, Miffy the ghost, from 'Miffy the ghost', 2001.

George Hendrik Breitner, 'Girl in a White Kimono', 1894; Rijksmuseum, Amsterdam; Mr and Mrs Drucker-Fraser Bequest, Montreux.
Dick Bruna, Miffy in kimono, autonomous work, 2008.

Hendrick Avercamp, 'Winter Landscape with Ice Skaters', c. 1608; Rijksmuseum, Amsterdam; purchased with the support of the Rembrandt Association.
Dick Bruna, Miffy skating, from 'Miffy in the snow', 1963.

Anonymous, 'Shiva Nataraja', Tamil Nadu, c. 1100–1200; Rijksmuseum, Amsterdam; on loan from the Royal Asian Art Society in the Netherlands.
Dick Bruna, Dancing, autonomous work, 1986.

Vincent van Gogh, 'Self-Portrait', 1887; Rijksmuseum, Amsterdam; gift of F.W.M., Baroness Bonger-van der Borch van Verwolde, Almen.
Dick Bruna, Farmer John, autonomous work, 1990.

Frits Koolhoven (design), 'FK 23 Double-Decker, named "Bantam"', 1918; Rijksmuseum, Amsterdam; purchased with the support of the M.B.T. de Groot Family/Rijksmuseum Fonds.
Dick Bruna, Miffy and Uncle Pilot, from 'Miffy goes flying', 1970.

Johannes Vermeer, 'The Milkmaid', c. 1658–1659; Rijksmuseum, Amsterdam; purchased with the support of the Rembrandt Association.
Dick Bruna, Miffy watering flowers, from 'Miffy's garden', 2004.

Adriaen Coorte, 'A Bowl of Strawberries on a Stone Plinth', 1696; Rijksmuseum, Amsterdam; transfer to the State in lieu of inheritance tax.
Dick Bruna, Strawberry, from 'I can do more sums', 1980.

Simon Maris, 'Isabella', c. 1906; Rijksmuseum, Amsterdam; A. van Wezel Bequest, Amsterdam.
Dick Bruna, Miffy wearing her tulip dress, autonomous work, 1997.

Henriëtte Ronner, 'Cat at Play', c. 1860–1878; Rijksmuseum, Amsterdam; J.B.A.M. Westerwoudt Bequest, Haarlem.
Dick Bruna, Cat, from 'Moo says the cow', 1995.

Anonymous, 'Ceremonial Chain of the Guild of Saint George of Zevenbergen', Breda, c. 1520–1541; Rijksmuseum, Amsterdam; purchased with the support of H.B. van der Ven, The Hague.
Dick Bruna, Mayor, from 'I am a clown', 1974.

Melchior d'Hondecoeter, 'Seven Chicks', c. 1665–1668; Rijksmuseum, Amsterdam; purchased with the support of the M. van Poecke Family and private collectors/Rijksmuseum Fonds.
Dick Bruna, Chicken with chicks, from 'I can count', 1968.

Rembrandt van Rijn, 'Officers and Other Civic Guardsmen of District II in Amsterdam, under the Command of Captain Frans Banninck Cocq and Lieutenant Willem van Ruytenburch', known as 'The Night Watch', 1642; Rijksmuseum, Amsterdam; on loan from the City of Amsterdam.
Dick Bruna, Miffy dances with friends and family, autonomous work, 2002.

Anonymous, 'Temple Guardian', Japan, c. 1300–1400; Rijksmuseum, Amsterdam; purchased with the support of the BankGiro Lottery, the M.J. Drabbe-fonds/Rijksmuseum Fonds, made available by ABN-AMRO, the Mondriaan Fund and the Rembrandt Association, with additional funding from the Cultuurfonds.
Dick Bruna, Knight, autonomous work, 1993.

Giambattista Moroni, 'Portrait of a Young Woman', 1560–1578; Rijksmuseum, Amsterdam; purchased with the support of the Rembrandt Association.
Dick Bruna, Poppy Pig takes a picture, from 'Grunty Pig and Miffy's ears', 2011.

Thérèse Schwartze, 'Young Woman, with "Puck" the dog', c. 1885–1886; Rijksmuseum, Amsterdam; A.G. van Anrooy Bequest, Kampen.
Dick Bruna, Miffy with dog, autonomous work, 1991.

Jozef Israëls, 'Children of the Sea', 1872; Rijksmuseum, Amsterdam; J.B.A.M. Westerwoudt Bequest, Haarlem.
Dick Bruna, Miffy on the beach, from 'Miffy at the seaside', 1963.

Étienne-Maurice Falconet, 'Seated Cupid', 1757; Rijksmuseum, Amsterdam; on loan from the Koninklijk Kabinet van Schilderijen Mauritshuis, The Hague.
Dick Bruna, Miffy loses her balloon, from 'Aunt Alice's party', 1992.

Front cover
Photo Rijksmuseum: John Lewis Marshall
Dick Bruna, Miffy looking at art, from 'Miffy at the gallery', 1997.

Back cover
Dick Bruna, At school, autonomous work, 1984.

This book was published in celebration of Miffy's 70th anniversary in 2025.

Text
Mercis Publishing bv

Translation
Richard de Nooy

Illustrations
Dick Bruna © copyright Mercis bv, 1953–2025

Images
Image Department of the Rijksmuseum

Design
Irma Boom Office

Lithography and Printing
Wilco Art Books, Amersfoort

Publishers
Mercis Publishing bv Amsterdam
Rijksmuseum Amsterdam

Mercis Publishing bv
Johannes Vermeerplein 3
1071 DV Amsterdam
The Netherlands

info@mercis.nl
nijntje.nl

Rijksmuseum
PO Box 74888
1070 DN Amsterdam
The Netherlands

publicaties@rijksmuseum.nl
rijksmuseum.nl

© copyright 2025 Mercis Publishing bv Amsterdam and Rijksmuseum Amsterdam

All rights reserved. No part of this publication may be reproduced, stored in a retrieval system, or transmitted in any form, or by other means, electronic or otherwise, without the prior written permission of the publisher.

ISBN 978-90-5647-155-2
10 9 8 7 6 5 4 3 2 1

Printed and bound in the Netherlands